For: Carroll, Ginger and Jack
Amy, Alice Elizabeth and Ty,
the next generations

If my words did glow with the gold of sunshine
And my tunes were played on the harp unstrung,
Would you hear my voice come though the music,
Would you hold it near as it were your own?

RIPPLE
The Grateful Dead

flexibility

I want to be
like prairie grass
tall supple,
swaying
with the breeze.

I want to be
like grains of sand
kissed, tossed
by ocean waves
to bask in sunlight,
 then pulled back
to rest beneath
the sea.

I want to be
flexible
 stop, turn,
face what
 calls to me

I want to be
present
to meet
each moment
of this one
and
   only
      life.

Preface

Resilience is accepting your new reality, even if it's less good than the one you had before. You can fight it, you can do nothing but scream about what you've lost, or you can accept that and try to put together something that's good.

Elizabeth Edwards

At times in my life, my heart has been broken open to the heart of others and that of the world. I have discovered this openheartedness allows everyday beauty and the magnitude of each moment to become a lens through which one experiences everyone, every event and every living thing.

The gospel tell us in the story of Jesus healing two blind men that our sight shall be returned. My sight has been returned through death. Death, my own near death, the death of beloved family members and friends and the unexpected death of my son, has opened the door to new life for me. I understand my experiences with death to be my own resurrection.

Through writing and offering myself fully to my life, I believe I am putting together something good. I continually turn more and more toward solitude, meditation, the healing forces of nature, the call of my ancestors and the suffering of others.

I am grateful to my writing community that faithfully and regularly convenes to listen to each other's words. I am thankful for my teachers who continue to guide me along this path and to those who sit with me on a regular basis in silent meditation. I know that together we are lifting collective consciousness and allowing the world and ourselves space needed for transformation.

I thank my husband who patiently allows me time alone to put words on paper. I thank my daughter, my daughter-in-law and grandchildren for accepting my craziness and laughing and for allowing me to be who I am. I am deeply thankful for friendship, for it is through many relationships and intimate fellow pilgrims that I continue to live into who I was designed to be.

As an elder I believe the most important gifts I have to leave behind are my Stories, and as best I can remember, stories of those who have gone before me. We stand on each other's shoulders. The stories of my life are proof of that. Without all the other lives that comprise my stories, I would not be here today. I am supported by innumerable others who have preceded me and those who stand beside me now. I know I cannot do this work of living without relationship.

This is a collection of my stories. The poems and reflections included throughout this book are mine unless attributed to another author. This is my gift to my beloveds. If you are reading this, you are one of them. This is my gift to you.

Morning

I awaken gently
easing
into dawn
just as darkness
fades.

Sunlight filters
through branches,
bouncing
off rooftops.

A chameleon debuts,
brown, blending
into the porch rail.

With wonder I watch,
in reverence
I bow
to the day.

Contents

EPIPHANY	1
GOODBYES	5
RESPONSIVENESS	13
FAMILY	19
CAMPFIRES	25
HOME	34
SURRENDER	39
ENDINGS	43
REFUGE	46
TRAGEDY	54
KULEANA	66
COMMUNION	74
SLOWING	81
CRUCIFIXION	88
FORGETFULNESS	92
WRITING	97
OPENHEARTEDNESS	101
IMAGINATION	110
DARKNESS	115
GIFTS	123
RELATIONSHIP	129
ROBASHIN	134

Epiphany

Epiphany is not a blazing light—
Epiphany is the chorus of rebels,
beggars, lunatics, bellowing with
your voice, the flickering revelations
that the words of the song in my head
are your words.

                              Martin Espada, poet

As I begin to write this it is two years and one week since my forty-year-old son, Trey, died suddenly of a massive heart attack on Christmas Eve of 2010. Now it is the eve of Epiphany, January 6, the day the Christian church remembers the three wise kings who followed a star to the manger of Jesus.

After presenting gifts to the infant king of the Jews who was born at a time and in a place proclaimed by the prophets, the kings, having been warned in a dream and recognizing the child as the Messiah, chose not to follow King Herod's instructions to return to him and reveal the place where Jesus could be found.

In the gospel of Matthew, on seeing the star, the kings are described as, "filled with delight." They are changed from within. They leave the Holy Family following a new path home guided by the magnitude of their deep felt experience. Webster defines Epiphany as a sudden manifestation of perception of the essential nature or meaning of something: an intuitive grasp of reality through something such as an event usually simple and striking.

On January 6, 2013, I attended the housewarming party of friends. The week prior, I pondered whether or not I would accept the invitation. I am more reluctant now to commit to events of more than just a few people, a pattern that seems to have emerged from grief and aging. "Chasing conversation" in large groups now requires more energy that I am willing to relinquish.

I always try to determine my intent. Like the kings I seek to follow the star. Now in the season of elderhood old routes no longer suffice. I am guided along new and different paths.

I have discovered that Epiphanies are outcomes of love exchanges. As I left the housewarming that day, the host offered me a candle and small stone. I was invited to make a New Year's wish or intent, drop the stone in the nearby creek, then take the candle home as a reminder of my wish. A friend asked me to join him in this ritual.

We crossed the street and stood in silence on a bridge overlooking the stream. I tossed my stone. My friend tossed his. Each offering pierced the still water's surface. Together we watched circles continuously appear and merge, symbols of our unending connectedness to each other and all of life.

In the reverence of the moment, I felt myself move toward acceptance. I experienced an opening beckoning me to step into my life as it is.

After so many mornings of waking and asking myself: "Did this really happen?" I now know this is my life: just this, here and now. My choice is to endure it or live it fully. At times I forget this choice ever before me, but for the most part I believe I have chosen to turn toward my life as it is one moment, one day at a time.

What We Know

I am going to die.
You know that, don't you?
So are you.
That is why this is important:
there must be no frivolous conversations,
no wasted moments of connection,
no lost words, touches,
smiles or tears.
There is no time to spare.

Goodbyes

As we live, we are transmitters of life.
And when we fail to transmit life, life
fails to flow through us.— it means
kindling the life-quality where it was not.

D.H. Lawrence

This was not the first time my sister and I were told this could be the end of our mother's life. On another occasion a few years prior Mother described to me a dream she had while in the hospital.

"Jesus was coming to meet me," she said. "He walked toward me with arms open. As He came nearer I turned around and ran back. I told Him I was not ready yet."

Those words, "not ready yet," now sound familiar. "Wait a minute," I often think. "How did I reach this place in my life with so much left to do and so little time?"

When I arrived at my mother's bedside in the hospital ICU, I knew this time was different. She lay hooked up to monitors and feeding tubes. I sensed her 94-year-old body failing.

As I sat with her, she asked that I read aloud. I picked up the book she was reading, Barack Obama's, *DREAMS OF MY FATHER*, and began.

"No, I have read that part," she said, so I moved ahead until I found her place and continued reading. After a few minutes I knew she was drifting to sleep.

"I am going now. I will be back in the morning," I whispered. As always she said, "I love you honey. I am so glad you are here." I left with certainty I would see her again.

I stayed alone at her home that night. I wanted to be with familiar sounds and smells of her and my imaginings of her walking down the hall on her walker in the morning. I always heard it touch the floor with each step she took, a click-click rhythm of its metal legs on the carpet. She would stop at my door peeking in to see if I was awake.

There are times in life when everything shifts. One of those times occurred for me when the phone rang around 5 a.m. the following morning. I picked up the receiver and heard the ICU nurse's gentle voice inform me that my mother had stopped breathing.

My mother's death was the first in a series of unexpected life-changing events during the next five years that would alter my world completely, after which I would never again look at each day, each person or event in my life in the same ways as before. I understand now that from the moment I emerged from my mother's womb I began my journey toward my own death.

Our Western culture prefers not to acknowledge that we walk daily hand in hand with death. Life teaches me the importance of embracing death as a transition to move and grow toward. Together, life and death create the mysterious completion of the unending cycle of creation.

The day of my mother's death I wrote:

> *Death is an open door drawing us into the light.*
> *Curious, but reluctant, we step forward. Slowly*
> *the pace increases, as we move toward openness,*
> *sensing some magnetic force drawing*
> *us closer until we run anticipating a return to*
> *the eternal embrace, peacefully, safely home.*

The deep beauty of the cycle of life began becoming apparent to me in a very real way when a few months after my mother's death, I joined my family at her island home. Her children, grandchildren and great-grandchildren stood together on a cliff on Kauai overlooking the Pacific and said our final "Alohas." Caressed by Hawaiian breezes, we released her ashes to the ocean.

For the first time in my life I began to experience grief as a process. I learned that grief left unacknowledged results in a sort of death of our own, limiting us in experiencing life fully here and now. I acknowledged great waves of sadness and memories both painful and joyful.

With the guidance of a friend and teacher, I was gradually able to integrate grief into my life. I did not allow myself to return to my daily routine as if nothing significant had happened.

I am the eldest child in my family. I accept this responsibility with humility and reverence. I am now a bridge from my mother's generation to the next two generations of our family. My father died when I was 27. My mother was with me until I was 66. She taught me many things that I shared in my tribute to her at her memorial service: be flexible, stand up straight, be positive, say the blessing, be a blessing, read the paper, read books, listen to music, challenge your mind, spark your imagination, be curious, don't give up---never, never, never give up!

I entered a new phase of my life as I said goodbye to her with these words from Isaiah 55:22:

> *For you shall go out in joy and be led back in peace. The mountains and hills before you shall burst into song and all the trees of the fields shall clap their hands.*

I Am

*I emerged from
your womb.
From darkness
into light
I was born,
took my first breath,
was given a name.*

*We danced
hand in hand,
then twirled apart
to solo,
no longer one,
but two.*

*Suddenly
you were gone.
I was alone.*

*I called for you.
In dreams I heard
you answer.*

*Because of you
I am no longer two
but one.*

The Shawl

I am wrapped
in my mother's
shawl.
Soft, white silky
threads
enfold me,
a comforting cocoon.
Fringe tickles
my arms.
I smile at memories
sitting alone
secure,
serene
wrapped in
my mother's
shawl.

Responsiveness

*What next? Why ask? Next will come a
demand about which you already know
all you need to know: that its sole measure
is your own strength.*

Dag Hammarskjold

Next for me is transmitting my stories to future generations. I now acknowledge that my stories are all I truly am.

As I near my 75th birthday, I recognize my life connects lives spanning more than a century: the generations of my great-grandparents, my grandparents, my parents, my children and my grandchildren.

In their book, *The Coming Interspiritual Age*, Kurt Johnson and David Ord point out that around 300 million years ago the amniotic egg evolved into being allowing the laying of eggs as protection and nurturing for the fully developed emergence of the next generation. I am hopeful that through transmitting stories, elders can turn toward aging as an opportunity to become the generational egg in which future generations might be protected and nurtured by wisdom prior to emerging fully developed as mature adults. It is true grown-ups that the world desperately needs today. To offer that which can come forth with aging is our opportunity to gift those who follow us with wise maturity, which is something far beyond simply aging.

It is my hope to continue to grow in wisdom and to be able to pass that wisdom on to the next generation. The hope I want to contribute to is an action word and something we must move toward together. If we do not take this action now, there is a tremendous possibility the opportunity will never come again.

Cynthia Borgeault tells us in *Mystical Hope* that hope's home is at the center of all creation as aliveness. This hope is a truth that when we are attuned to it, sends us forth no matter what the outward circumstances of our lives.

As elders I believe we must begin our work by facing our grief: the grief of aging, of losing loved ones, of fully facing death, the underlying grief for what is happening to our institutions, our political foundations, our families, our children, our planet, our mother, the earth. I have discovered what it is to turn toward grief. I have learned, with the help and guidance of many others, the importance of facing life's unexpected events and following them toward transformation.

In the process of facing grief, I have become aware of unacknowledged sorrow we are experiencing collectively as human beings on planet earth. In spite of all that seems uncertain in our lives, we can learn together that grief turned toward and acknowledged can give us strength and courage to propel us forward in new directions.

In an interview, Kathleen Dean Moore, Distinguished Professor of Philosophy at Oregon State University, refers to the ferocious love of a grandmother. I have referred to this fierceness of maternal love in writing through grief over my son's death. I have witnessed the unrelenting watchfulness and nurtured guidance of ferocious love express itself in innumerable ways through many forms in nature.

It isn't enough to love a child and wish her well. It isn't enough to open my heart to a bird-graced morning. Can I claim to love a child if I don't use all the power of my breathing heart to preserve a world that nourishes children's joy? Loving is not a kind of la-de-da. Loving is a sacred trust. To love is to affirm the absolute worth of what you love and to pledge your life to its thriving---to protect it fiercely and faithfully for all times.

> *Moral Ground: Ethical Action for a Planet in Peril*
> Kathleen Dean Moore and
> Michael P. Nelson, eds.

I receive these words as a challenge and a responsibility. It is now time for me to fully devote my energy to the task of healing in whatever ways I may be called to do so. It is my time to respond in hope with my life experiences and wisdom as my gift to those who follow me.

The Request

"Hypnotize me!"
my granddaughter commanded
as we lay in the old iron bed
on the screened-in porch
one summer night.

" How would I do that?"

"With a clock that goes back and forth."

"A metronome?
You don't need that.
Look at silhouettes
of cypress branches
swaying
in the breezes.
Listen to frog symphonies
and cricket serenades.
Let your imagination wander with
the flow
of the creek.

*Be guided by fireflies.
Watch moon's beams
dancing
through the woods.
You will be hypnotized,
dear one,
by wonder!"*

Family

*"Real isn't how you are made," said
the skin horse. "It's a thing that
happens to you."*

> Margery Williams
> *The Velveteen Rabbit*

My childhood summers in Texas meant time on my grandparents' ranch with my sister and four cousins. After mornings of play in the openness, we spent the hours of midday high heat inside.

The young ones would lie in big iron beds on the back porch and nap. The older ones, my cousin Jay and me, were allowed to rest and read lying on a quilt pallet on the living room floor beneath the ceiling fan.

The earth and books were my home for as long as I can remember. I retreated daily into my imagination through the pages of books my grandmother ordered weekly from the library in Kilgore. Tom would drive through the piney woods on the two lane highway to check on things at the big house there and pick up a new supply of books.

Tom was the black man who worked for my grandparents throughout my childhood and until I was a young adult. We did not call Tom a houseman or a hired hand as some people did in those days. Tom was family.

As I write I see his face as vividly as if he were here beside me. Tom brought our luggage in when we arrived at my grandparents' for a visit. He fixed our meals. He helped keep the house clean. He was always there for us.

Once I fell off my horse as it galloped into the yard and came to an abrupt halt. I hit my head on a brick, knocking me dizzy. It was Tom who bolted out the door, helped me inside to lie on the couch and brought a cold cloth for my head.

It was Tom who cooked up those huge farm dinners as we referred to our noon meal back then—fried chicken, mashed potatoes, corn, fresh hot rolls with butter, iced tea and of course the desserts—pound cake, blackberry cobbler, homemade ice cream. It was Tom who carefully arranged leftovers on the back of the kitchen stove for us to sneak a snack from and make a plate of supper. I was always amazed at how good the noon meal could taste and that leftovers seemed even better!

It was Tom who in the mornings left the kitchen door ajar so the two of us could visit while he served my breakfast. Then when my grandmother arrived in the breakfast room, he softly slid the door shut and waited until she beckoned him. It was Tom who brought fresh flowers from the garden for my grandmother to arrange. It was Tom who, when I turned 12, began calling me Miss Judy and I knew something had changed. On one hand I felt proud and grown up, and on the other I felt I was giving up something I was not ready to relinquish.

Tom was part of our family. There was an unwritten understanding about that. We all recognized that we were family, each and every one of us.

It was Tom who would leave one day with books that were due and faithfully return the next with many new selections. When I saw the cloud of dust appear down the road on days I knew he would be arriving back at the farm, I would be in the driveway to meet him and help carry in the load of books that I could not wait to read.

On those summer afternoons I lost myself in biographies of early American heroes, *Little House on the Prairie, The Bobbsey Twins, Tom Sawyer, Huckleberry Finn, Heidi, Treasure Island* and many others. Often the stories we read became themes for our play in the hayloft, the open pastures and at the pond where we swam daily after walking single file down the dusty road, my mother leading and my aunt, Shirley, bringing up the rear.

The stories allowed us to become anything we wished—cowboys, Alpine princesses, vagabonds off on adventures that in one way or another allowed total freedom in the natural world.

That was where I belonged, close to the earth and smells of growing and alive things or lost in words that filled my imagination with constant new wonders. It was a beautiful childhood in spite of underlying adult conflicts that even in my child world I knew were taking place. Still, the magic of a farm with grandparents, fresh milk, watermelon, sprinklers to run through, horses to ride, jack rabbits to chase, fish to catch, totally overshadowed everything else so that deep down no matter what else was going on, I knew that I was loved.

Summer Storms

*Powerful storms sometimes
blow up out of nowhere.
I remember the force of
a furious wind
when moments before
the air was calm.
Instantly everything changed.
We ran to the cellar,
that dark, damp underground place
that smelled of dirt and roots.
My grandfather carried a kerosene lantern
leading the way.
We hurried down
wooden steps---
my grandmother, my mother, my sister and me.
My grandfather slammed the hinged door shut,
then hurried back into darkness.
I was terrified he would not return,
but he did, just as pounding rain let loose
and the storm's rage increased.
We huddled together protected
down in the earth
with my grandmother's jars of green beans,*

black-eyed peas and pickled peaches.
Not one fell off the shelf or broke.
Earth, our mother, held us
until the uproar subsided.
We emerged from hiding safe and whole.
The Chinaberry tree by the back door,
was left twisted and broken.
For months I could not look at it.
Each time I hurried out that door
I hid my face in my hands
until I passed the wounded tree.
The sight of it
was more than I could bear.

Campfires

*I know what you have to experience before
you die; let me tell you. What you have to
experience before you die is a driving rain
transformed into light—what it means to die;
when we disappear, it is the others who die for us,
—And then, an illumination—but inside the sun.*

> Muriel Barbery
> *The Elegance of the Hedgehog*

I recall campfires of my childhood in the East Texas piney woods where my family lived. Many weekend mornings, my father built a fire and followed his ritual of campfire cooking.

I remember smells of bacon frying and how he would take thick pieces of bread, dip it in bacon grease and grill it over the coals, then scramble eggs in the black cast iron skillet. When everything was ready, it was piled onto one big platter for us to help ourselves from.

Often other families joined us for these outdoor breakfasts. The children played in the openness of the yard and pasture while grown ups sat around lingering flames, drinking coffee and visiting.

My daddy with his great Irish sense of humor told jokes and laughter rang out across the outdoors. His simple stories added gentle humor into everyday conversation. He had a gift for joining people together in laughter with his sly grin and twinkling eyes.

As I grew older my family stories changed. My father, the outdoor cook and humorist, was an alcoholic. He died of alcoholism. My mother was a hardworking, positive thinking, determined Texas woman who tried to control my father's drinking and failed.

As my father's disease progressed through the years, my family life became increasingly unpredictable, sometimes chaotic. Later in my own adult life I, too, became an alcoholic, the one thing I said I would never allow to happen. But it did. Now having lived the 12 Step Program of Alcoholics Anonymous for almost three decades, I have come to a different understanding of myself, my family and my stories.

I have done the dying for my parents so that their essence, the sun inside them, is all that now lives within me. It is the light of their lives I choose to let shine in my heart and to pass on to future generations.

Years ago I learned through my 12 Step Program and spiritual teachers I trusted, "you can change the story," the same message I once saw printed boldly on a billboard along Interstate 40.

In the beginning stages of living this message, I remember thinking, "How do I write a new script? How do I write my way through pain and disappointment as if the causes of those things never happened?" But that is not how my stories changed. They changed by my living my life one day at a time and following my true path as faithfully as possible. I did not change my stories. I changed and everything else changed with me. I believe it is called transformation.

The sun in my father's life shone through in simple lessons of how to commune with family and friends in laughter, to see surprises and how to build a campfire.

When my children were young, we participated in the family ritual my father taught me. When we are all together now, though one is missing, me, my daughter, my four grandchildren, three generations of us, build our fires, tell our stories and sing our songs. There is magic and intimacy in sharing ourselves with each other in the brilliance of firelight.

Recently I sat near the fireplace with my friend in her home. In those moments, I believe we became more aware of who we each are and what was emerging from our encounter. We were in that glowing sacred space of communion. In the brilliance of a fire I feel a great freedom allowing new possibilities of life to burst forth and announce themselves in spontaneous flying sparks of light.

Campfires

*We gathered branches and sticks
we called kindlin',
scooped handfuls of dry leaves,
all bits and pieces
fallen from trees
in the woods.*

*We built our campfire.
Striking matches
one, by, one,
blowing quick breaths,
we fanned sparks
'til flames
danced against
the evening sky.*

*Shadows played through trees.
We sat near the edge
of the fire,
faces glowing, we shared tall tales
and joined our voices in melodies.*

Mesmerized by mystery,
we watched
as smoke

ribbons
swirled
into
the
night.

Catfish

My daddy liked to fish.
He often escaped to the pond
on my grandfather's farm.
He'd cast his hook
from a bamboo pole
in hopes of catching catfish.

Who would mess around
with such slimy things?
Not me!

But I did like to eat them
fried up crisp
in cornmeal batter,
soft, juicy and sweet to taste,
washed down with iced tea
on a hot summer day.

There's no use imagining
I could cook catfish
or want to.
I'm sticking to walking
in the woods,

*throwing off my clothes,
jumping into the water.*

*Through all these years
no amount of knowledge
has made me change my ways!*

Connection

Flashing campfire flames,
dancing wonder,
smells of cedar
burning, crackling,
    shooting sparks skyward,
grabbed by gravity
sizzling to ashes,
floating homeward
becoming earth again.

Sitting together
    circling
glowing embers
children softly sing,
firelight flashing
in their eyes.

Home

You can't connect the dots looking forward. You can only connect them looking backwards. So you have to trust in something: your gut, destiny, life, karma, whatever. Because believing that the dots will connect down the road will give you the confidence to follow your heart, even when it leads you off the well worn path.

                        Steve Jobs

Late June was the beginning of hay harvesting season on my grandfather's ranch in East Texas. As a child I was fascinated watching this process. First, the big gas-powered mower swept through the pastures leveling tall stalks of ripened alfalfa. Freshly mowed hay then lay on the ground for a couple of days, drying in the sun before baling began.

Next, raking machines appeared moving through the pasture, picking up hay and stacking it into long flowing windrows. When raking was completed, the entire field appeared to be a giant golden maze. Hay rows reflected summer's sun, the light seemingly bouncing across the field in one continuous dance.

The baler itself most attracted my attention. Pulled by a tractor it had wire-like teeth in front that picked up hay, feeding it into the baling chamber to be compressed into rectangular-shaped bales. Each was then automatically tied securely with two sets of taut wire. The bales were loaded onto a wagon and transported to the barn, then lifted into the loft and stored in neatly stacked patterns until needed for winter livestock feeding.

I was too young to help with the baling process but I loved to saddle my Shetland pony, Stardust, ride to the nearby pasture and watch. I would head out the back door ready for the day with my grandmother calling behind me, "Don't forget your head gear!"

Just inside the kitchen entrance were hooks along the wall that held straw hats of all shapes and sizes. Reluctantly I grabbed one, put it on my head and pulled the drawstring tight so as not to lose it on my ride. Most every morning I headed toward the barn to saddle my gentle pony with her brown coat, big brown eyes, dark mane and a white star-like mark in the center of her forehead from which I took her name.

I remember one day after saddling up, I rode down the dusty road in the lake pasture until I reached the baling machine already in full throttle. My grandfather's work crew loaded hay bales with the constant noise of machinery filling the background. I guided Stardust as near the baler as possible so I could get a close look at what was going on.

Then before I knew what was happening I was headed home at high speed. Reacting to the continued noise or some unexpected movement the horse shied, quickly did an about-turn and took off at her fastest canter. Instinctively I attempted to restrain the pony, pulling fiercely on the reins without results. I finally just held on tightly for the ride the reins held loosely, my hands gripping the saddle horn, my legs grabbing Stardust's circumference as tightly as possible and my heels down securely in the stirrups. I had no choice other than to allow this ride to take me where it would.

Down the pasture road we flew, through the gate, a sharp left turn and I knew we were headed home. With my straw hat flying behind me we did not stop, as we raced past the barn on our way to the big front porch of the farmhouse.

Arriving at her destination, Stardust halted abruptly, stomped both front feet and let out a relieved whinny. My grandparents, sitting on the porch, looked up at us amazed.

"You must be in a hurry today!" my grandfather said. "Oh, I just wanted to see how fast she could get me home," I replied as casually as possible hoping they would not suspect that actually this ride was not one of my choosing, but rather that of Stardust's, who was determined to get us home from whatever she feared as quickly as possible.

As often as possible, I visit a young friend who has stage 4 melanoma. I have known her 11 years since I had her oldest child in my class at the preschool where I teach. She also has two younger children, twins, a boy and a girl, a devoted husband and a mother who is at her side daily, a mother who just a few years earlier lost her only other child, a son.

It seems Elizabeth and her struggle is never really out of my mind. I don't pray for one outcome or another. I don't know how to do that. I do know how to hold her in this light I now know intimately. I do know how to give her to the light. I do know it is all I know to do. I do know like my pony, Elizabeth is heading home as all of us are. My hope is hers, I do believe, and that is somehow she will know like Stardust when it is time to let go, allowing fear to become the fearlessness that propels her swiftly and surely until she comes to rest having finally reached home.

My Wish

*I wish
that I could give you
wings to fly
into the darkness
of the morning
where you
would meet the dawn
and become it— translucent,
swimming in the glow
of pure existence,
utter beauty,
unfettered joy,
unbounded love!*

Surrender

*A human being is part of the whole,
called by us the universe: a part limited
by time and space. He experiences himself,
his thoughts, and feelings as something
separated from the rest, a kind of optical illusion
of consciousness. This delusion is a kind of prison
for us, restricting us to our personal desires and
to affection for a few persons nearest us. Our task is
to free ourselves from this prison.*

Albert Einstein

Grief changes us. I have read that experiencing and allowing one's self to be fully in touch with deep grief and trauma opens us up to ourselves, the world, the mystery. We begin to evolve into who we truly are.

I have discovered I can and cannot make this journey alone. As isolated as I have felt and sometimes still do, I continue to exist in this time and space as part of the whole manifested as a human being. In many ways grief has turned me toward my own longings.

I have established a daily writing practice. I have always known writing to be my best means of communication. I write to share myself with the world because in spite of all its flaws, its disappointments, its seeming misguidedness, it is a beautiful world, and I love it. I love its natural beauty, a realm I turn to again and again for comfort and renewal. I love its people, even those who seem difficult to me at times. I know they are my greatest teachers.

I sit down every day and write something as a gift to myself and those who recognize my writing is from the heart. Through this practice, my grief is transformed into joy that I release and send forth in its miraculous newness.

My young friend, Elizabeth, died. During the last two weeks of her life I often sat with her at Christopher House, our Hospice house here in Austin. The room was airy and bright. There was a large window near her bed and double doors opening out onto a private patio.

At times Elizabeth would hear wind chimes in the trees just outside. I sat rubbing her feet and watching her slow breaths, wondering if the next one was going to come.

The last few days of her life I did not return to visit. I was depleted. I had to rest. A friend and teacher told me, "You must stop now and care for yourself. You are like a bird learning to fly that has run into a window and fallen on the ground."

Again, as so often happens for me, another gave words to what I was experiencing when I could not. I was able to let go and so did Elizabeth who soon moved peacefully into greater life.

Something

I felt it or I heard it.
It touched me or it whispered.
I turned to face it.
It was not there.
I saw a feather floating
lightly to the ground,
swirling
like the moment
of knowing and unknowing,
something I cannot say.

Endings

*As we live, we are transmitters of life,
and when we fail to transmit life, life fails
to flow through us.—it means kindling the
life-quality where it was not.*

                                                               D.H. Lawrence

FOUR DAYS

    1.   things we say:

*It is near the first day of spring, just two days away, in fact.
Outside the wind chime is singing.
Propped up on pillows, slowly turning toward the sounds,
you say, "It seems like cowbells," and we smile.*

*You say, "I like the color of your blouse, sage."
I say, "I usually wear a t shirt but since I was coming to see you
I wore something better!"
We laugh.*

*You say, "There is so much I want to express.
I am having trouble finding words."*

*I say, "We don't have to talk.
Let's just be here together."
So we sit in silence,
me at the foot of your bed rubbing your feet.*

*I know you are leaving, that even now
you are on your way.*

*When our visit ends, I don't say, "Good-bye."
I just say, "See you soon,"
because I know I will.*

    2.   the next day

*How fragile the thread between life and death.
I see you lying there like a feather that has softly
drifted in with the breeze
not knowing when or where it will land,
just trusting its existence and the journey.
I whisper in your ear. Your eyelids flutter.
You rest again in that thin place
where the fullness of wisdom sits
waiting to welcome you home.*

3. afterwards:

*When I am overwhelmed by grief,
my own, that of my loved ones and the world,
I sit on my rock overlooking the river and wait.*

*I wait 'til the river flows right up through me,
'til the violet sunset glows against the hills,
'til bird songs become less frequent
then fade into dusk.*

*I sit in early evening silence to be filled again
with hope arriving on wings of wonder
hitching a ride on the first evening star!*

4. unraveling:

*At times when my world unravels
and life as I know it appears
to be falling apart,
I remember my mother after the celebration,
unraveling Christmas bows,
smoothing them gently,
then rolling them onto a spool
to save for tying on future gifts.
A child of the depression,
she passed on her belief
in constant new beginnings.*

Refuge

— It was an awe that smote and held him and, without seeing, he knew it could only mean that some august Presence was very, very near. With difficulty he turned to look for his friend, and saw him at his side cowed, stricken, and trembling violently. And still there was utter silence in the populous bird-haunted branches around them, and still the light grew and grew.

> Kenneth Grahame
> *The Wind in the Willows*

I do not recall when I first sought refuge in nature. As a young girl living with my family in the East Texas countryside, I would often head down the hill in front of our house into the hidden ravine where ferns, wild vines and seedling oaks provided a perfect nest. This was a "being place" for me. It was a the place of the hidden spring where minnows darted like tiny shadows through bubbling water.

Like Joseph, I was a dreamer. In school my teachers said, "pay attention." At home my mother said, "Are you listening to me?" Part of me was paying attention. Part of me was listening, but another part of me was out in the natural world riding horseback, climbing trees, splashing in cool creek waters. That better part of me was always lost in wonder.

In each new place I have lived I have always discovered a "being place." One of the first of these places was the tree house my father built for me. The little wooden house sat high in the branches of my favorite tree. I often retreated to my tree with favorite books and writing pads.

I spent many hours in this place of solitude. It was there I began learning the importance of just being, experiencing earth's beauty and the realm of imagination. I began to know the freedom of self-discovery through immersing myself in the arms of creation. I realized even then there was something much bigger, much grander than me. I began to know a Presence that could be trusted and could simply be called by one name, Love.

Through the years I have shared special "being places" with intimate loved ones. The times spent together in these place have deepened our relationships and sent us forth to meet our own lives more fully open to others and to the world.

I recall one early morning I sat in the park on an old wood bench where the trail begins and awaited a friend's arrival. Together we would greet the day in sounds of silence. As I waited a hummingbird entertained, darting about feeding on red salvia blossoms. I heard the bird that persistently sings, "Ju-dy, Ju-dy, Ju-dy!" A brisk spring breeze rustled through the trees. The peacock's mating call sounded out across the woods. I was alive with every living plant, creature, the sun, the sky, the clouds and the river. I remembered the words of a song I sing with the children: "All things bright and beautiful, all creatures great and small, all things wise and wonderful, the Lord God made them all."

Soon my friend arrived. We walked the dusty trail to a bench overlooking the river. We were held beneath a canopy of tree limbs laden with fresh spring growth framing the view to the water. Together we sat surrounded by the natural world: earth, water, sky, sun, plants, animals, birds. From deep within my heart I heard the words of Ezekiel 15:29, *"And I will give them a single heart and a new spirit I will put within them."* In those moments of contemplation we were changed individually and together, and the world around us was changed and the universe expanded more fully into love.

My Name

There is a bird
outside my window.
It is not the one
that says, "Ju-dy, Ju-dy, Ju-dy!"
I know I will hear that one soon.
He never fails
to sing good morning
calling out my name!

Oh, yes, I hear him now!

Uncertainty

*On the ridge above Cypress Creek
the screened porch waits,
its iron bed and straight-back chair
calling me to sit and listen
to the water below.*

*Cypress branches dance around me.
I hear your laughter,
see you drop from the rope swing,
break the water's surface,
wildly splash, eager for more.*

*In the front yard of this old log cabin
standing beneath the live oak tree
you and Amy exchanged wedding vows;
your father officiating,
me holding grandson, Jack.*

*Everyone we all loved most was there,
a real family wedding,
with an outdoor home cooked nuptial feast,
guitar music and foot stomping.*

*We waved sparklers in the night
as you and Amy
raced for the car
and headed out,
none of us suspecting
where the road
    would lead.*

White Swan

Out in the marsh,
the white swan,
her slender neck
stately stretched
skyward,
fluid eyes gazing
directly ahead,
black beak poised
ready to reach
for the catch,
sails across the water,
her great
   arched wings
      billowing,
filled with summer breezes,
   propelling
     her
        effortlessly
          on her way.

Refuge

I heard its call before I arrived.
When I found myself there,
something about the place knew me.
When it came time to leave,
I resisted.
This has happened again and again—
>*This call has lived forever*
>*in my soul.*

When I hear it,
I am certain
I am home.

Tragedy

There's no tragedy in life like the death of a child. Things never get back to the way they were.

Dwight Eisenhower

Age and grief seem to open a floodgate of memories. It is my memories that offer me hope. It is looking back that propels me forward. It is my personal stories of who I have been that move me into who I am now and the possibilities of who I might become:

The motorcade from Love Field was to follow a route into downtown Dallas I knew well. From Love Field the procession would head west on Mockingbird Lane, turn south on Lemmon, take Turtle Creek Blvd. and Cedar Springs, head into the downtown area, proceed on to Elm and then Stemmons Freeway and finally make its way to the Dallas Trade Center.

As usual, I drove a portion of that route to work the morning of November 22, 1963. I was headed to *The*

Dallas Times Herald newsroom where I worked as a young reporter. There was great excitement in the air, a heightened feeling of exhilaration that I sensed driving in to the city early that cool, cloudy fall morning.

Appropriately, by mid-morning the clouds broke and the sun shone forth just as Air Force One touched down at Love Field from Carswell Air Force Base in Fort Worth. As I drove in I noticed that portions of the motorcade route had been marked off and there were signs of security officers being stationed along the way.

I knew where many friends would be awaiting the arrival of President John F. Kennedy and the First Lady. Some would be at Love Field. Others would be at various points along the designated route to the Trade Center where a Democratic fundraising luncheon was to be held. It was a sold-out event for 2,600 people. The president would speak before the annual meeting of the Dallas Citizens Council. Now well into his third year as president, Kennedy was visiting Texas in an attempt to reunite our state's Democratic Party.

Dallas had voted Republican in the previous election. In October that year during his Dallas visit, Adlai Stephenson, then US Ambassador to the U.N., was met by angry right-wing demonstrators and hit on the head with a placard denouncing the U.N.

Stephenson advised Kennedy not to include Dallas in his Texas stops. The day before the president arrived,

"Wanted for Treason" posters of him were circulated on Dallas streets distributed by members of the John Birch Society who also paid for a full page, black bordered anti-Kennedy ad in *The Dallas Morning News* which ran the morning of November 22.

These are not facts about the city I grew up in and where my children were raised that I am proud to remember. I doubt, however, any of that was on the minds of those of us that day, as we headed for the newsroom of *The Dallas Times Herald*, the city's liberal evening paper.

Our thoughts were on the schedule for the day: the president was coming to Town, and we were ready. As Dallas' evening newspaper, the *Times Herald* would be the first newspaper in the country to publish the events of the day. As reporters for this paper we were participants in the day's events—even me who as one of the youngest reporters on staff would be among those remaining in the newsroom to take stories called in from all over town.

By 10 a.m. that morning the newsroom floor was clear except for a few of us. It was unusually quiet. I went to the windows facing south, the direction from which the motorcade would be approaching. Main Street was two blocks beyond the *Dallas Times Herald* offices, but peering through rows of buildings I could glimpse the street. I watched as crowds began gathering. Although I did not have a direct view I was able to determine where the entourage was in relation to the building I was in and when it proceeded moving past in the direction of Elm and the underpass that would take it onto Stemmons Freeway.

Soon after I returned to my desk, I clearly remember the phone on the City Editor's desk ringing. Felix McKnight, publisher and executive editor of the paper, was nearby and picked up the call. In a shocked voice I heard him cry out, "My God, the president has been shot!" as he slammed the receiver down. For the remainder of the day and into the night we took stories and interviewed people by phone. The first edition of the paper appeared as usual late that afternoon and was the first published account of JFK's assassination. The large bold black headline read:

JFK AMBUSHED IN DALLAS; PRESIDENT IS DEAD; CONNALLY SHOT.

Felix McKnight had made all press arrangements for President Kennedy's visit. I have wondered why he was on the newsroom floor when the first call came in. At heart I knew him as first and always a reporter. I assume he was on the newsroom floor making sure everyone was where he/she should be and tending to last minute details before leaving for the Dallas Trade Center.

I recall vividly the following 24 hours of pandemonium on the newsroom floor and in the 3rd floor corridor of the Dallas Police Headquarters where Oswald was taken after his arrest early that afternoon. Within that time span there were up to 800 representatives of news media in Dallas, including foreign correspondents and press association representatives.

Sometime in the early evening hours an out of town correspondent asked me to take him to the site of the tragedy. We went to Dealey Plaza to inspect the area. I looked up at the School Book Depository and the window from which the shots had been fired. I remember thinking I had never paid much attention to that building before and did not actually know what it was until that day.

Later I guided the reporter to Dallas Police Headquarters where with press passes we had no problem gaining entrance. By that time Oswald was already in custody and was being held on the 5th floor. We barely gained entrance to the 3rd floor corridor of the building as it was jammed with more than 100 news and camera personnel.

I do not know what time I returned home that night. I remember feeling lost, as if everything I had known before was totally unfamiliar. I was exhausted, not just physically but emotionally and spiritually. My world was, as was the world of a nation and a globe, completely altered.

I always had a clear view of happenings at *The Dallas Times Herald*. My desk on the newsroom floor was just across from Felix McKnight's glassed in office. From his desk chair he faced out into the newsroom and was always aware of what was happening. At any point in the day I could look into his office and wonder what he was working on. As a novice reporter I learned from him the power of words. Occasionally he would review a story with me and suggest words other than those I used. He explained how much could be said in one word enabling the reader to visualize and understand what the writer wished to convey.

He was much more to me than just my executive editor. I grew up across the street from him. His younger daughter, Ann, was one of my best friends growing up and throughout our adulthood until she died from cancer. She was godmother to my son, Trey. Her father was very influential in my majoring in journalism and becoming a reporter. Before he was my editor he was my friend, a father figure, my protector. He was one of those who my generation felt was supposed to somehow keep these tragic events from happening.

At the end of the day on Friday, November 22, 1963, a letter was posted in the newsroom. It was typed on personal stationery bordered with blue and orange and the name Felix R. McKnight printed on the top left corner. It was signed in blue ink.

It read:

Nov. 22

To The Staff:

Today you performed superbly.

No other newspaper in this country could have done a better job within the severe time limitations.

All of you took difficult assignments and came through without faltering.

It is a sad day.

I do not know what to say to you, except there should be no pride in a story such as this—except for the professional manner in which you labored with the same feeling of numbness that I had.

We must handle this story with the best of taste the next few days. We are sort of on trial because it happened in our city.

Thank you for being the wonderful people you are.

Felix McKnight

I write this as Dallas prepares to observe the 50th anniversary of Kennedy's assassination, and I reflect on many people referred to in his letter and their perseverance and courage in delivering news facts as clearly and precisely as possible. The journalistic ethics we observed in those days of simply presenting the facts accurately and honestly were brought forth in our coverage of this unexpected and tragic event.

I knew these heroes—Jim Lehrer, Bob Jackson, A.C. Greene, Blackie Sherrod, Darwin Payne, Vivian Castleberry— and I learned from them. They were my mentors. Because of them and many, many others including myself, who put aside shock and grief that day in order to provide as updated news as possible to a traumatized world, I will always remember this refrain:

Don't let it be forgot,
that once there was a spot
for one brief shining moment
that was known as Camelot.

Alan Jay Lerner

Meanings Within Meanings

The hawk sat on a tree limb
outside my window
silently watching
every movement
in the winter afternoon.

I thought it was an owl,
but it was not.

Some told me
not to lose
hope or faith
when my son
died
suddenly.

Hope for what?
Faith in what?
They did not know
what they were saying.

*Words that death
made real for me
like seeing a hawk
as an owl.*

Question

*It is near his birthday.
Facebook post this morning:
Amy and children in San Antonio,
standing on the bridge
where their daddy and mommy
stood the night before
he proposed.*

*Their lives move on now
as does mine.
The dead continue to die
I have read—*
      or do they?

Three Years Later

"Do you know that I sleep in
an old T shirt of Trey's.
It has a hole in it,
but it's soft and cozy,"
my granddaughter explained.

"I found it in a drawer of Mom's
with a Grateful Dead tie-dyed one."

What siblings keep of each other, I thought
as a tightness in my chest reminded me to breathe.

"We never know what comforts us
until we try it on," I said,
as I reached out to touch her hand.

Kuleana

HAWAIIAN PRAYER

May the earth continue to live,
May the heavens above continue to live,
May the rains continue to dampen the land,
May the wet forest continue to grow,
Then the flowers shall bloom
And we people shall live again.

Kuleana in Hawaiian means the freedom to tell your stories, to offer to others what has been given to you. In *kuleana* you are responsible for telling your story in the right way and at the right time so that it will flow out to others as an offering. In *kuleana* each story you tell will find its true listener, will land where it is intended to land because you are in *kuleana*.

Many years ago I stayed alone at our family home on the Island of Kauai. Early each morning I hiked the winding trail down the cliff to the sea.

One day as I strolled barefoot along the beach, the coarse black volcanic sand massaging my feet as I breathed in the beauty of my surroundings, I glanced toward a volcanic boulder standing stately near the shoreline. I was delighted to see a cowrie shell clinging to the side of the rock. I ran to examine the shell and reached out to claim it for my own but was surprised to discover I could not pry it loose.

Aloha 'aina means love of the land, respect for nature. Native Hawaiians traditionally ask permission and give thanks as the protocol that extends to every aspect of life in nature. In keeping with this tradition I repeated, "Please, thank you, please, thank you," as I hurried back up the cliff to the house for a knife to pry the shell loose, all the while hoping no one would come take it before I returned.

Back at the beach I found the shell still intact and began the task of retrieving it. Carefully I worked until I had the treasure in my hands. I watched as the creature it held quickly curled up and slipped deep inside its dark container of protection. It was then I considered the life the shell protected. It was this life that had attached itself to the lava rock. I needed to know my responsibility to the life itself before I claimed the shell.

The *keike* (native Hawaiian children) taught me. They showed me how to dig a hole in the red volcanic dirt, bury the shell and wait. They explained that soon ants would come to dig in the sand, then down into the shell to feed from its contents.

They were teaching me *e malana pono I ka 'aina, nana mai keola,* to take good care of the land as it grants life.

"What you take from earth, you must somehow return to earth before you do anything else," the children explained. They told me the shell was a gift from the earth but its contents and participation in the continuation of life was its gift back to the earth which it needed to make.

"You must leave it with earth until the ants have helped it fulfill its purpose," they instructed.

I asked how long that would be. I wanted to know the shell would be ready for me to take home when it was time to leave the island.

"A week or so, be patient, you will see," they said.

I followed their directions and buried the shell in the hard red earth. Soon ants arrived and dug into the volcanic soil. I watched for days until there were fewer and fewer ants and I knew it must be time to retrieve my precious shell. I dug it up and sure enough the shell was empty.

As further instructed I washed and cleaned the treasure, then carefully rubbed it with oil bringing forth its distinct colors and designs.

"The patterns on its back," the *keike* told me, "tell its story. "The opening underneath is the entrance to its secrets. Hold it to your ear. It will tell you its tales," they said.

I did as they told me. Then my children did the same. Now my grandchildren listen to the cowrie shell teach that all life is connected—everything, everyone, all we hold sacred is part of everything else.

This gift from the sea sits on my home altar where I see it every day. During the past few years I have come to know through experience that life is fragile and can take unwanted turns at unexpected moments. However difficult these experiences have been, they have taught me all creation is held in a Divine Embrace like the embrace of the cowrie shell held by the sea, that gave it to the lava rock that kept it safely for me.

The native children came to me to lead me in the process of bringing the shell home to further teach new generations its gift of wholeness. When I look at it now, I remember my delight on first discovering the shell and sensing it would be mine.

Cowrie shells are not easily found on the beaches of Kauai. I felt then and do now this shell is special, a gift to me from the universe.

I treasure my cowrie shell. It came to me at a time of great change in my life.

Then in my late 40s I had recently gotten sober and joined the program of Alcoholics Anonymous. I had come to Kauai alone to reflect on this personal passage and to be filled with the beauty and peace of the island—the Aloha spirit.

The unexpected appearance of the cowrie shell symbolized change, possibility and a newness of life. I respect the cowrie shell as a sacrament, which the Christian church defines as an "outward and visible sign of an inward and spiritual grace." To me the shell is a material symbol of something holy and sacred—a sacrament given by and received in grace.

> *Split wood, I am there. Lift up a rock,*
> *you will find me there.*
>
> The Gospel of Thomas, 77b

A Poem Of Hawaiian Proverbs

Aia no I ke ko a keau
Which ever way the current goes

He manu ke aloha 'a 'ohe lala kau 'ole
Love is like a bird—there is no branch
that it does not perch upon.

Malu ke kula, o'ohe ke 'u pueo
All is at peace.

Nolowale i ka 'ehu o ke kai
Lost in sea sprays

Ola I ke ahe lau makani
There is life in a gentle breath.

    trans. *by* MARY KAWENA PUKUI

Mount Wai'ale'ale

A new day emerges.
Faint light appears
as sun rays rim
*   the horizon.*

Creation continues.

Dark silhouettes,
earth's upheavals,
rise upward toward
the sky.
Misty clouds ascend
obscuring portions of
the mountain's chiseled face.

Rain droplets linger
urging tropical growth,
then rise floating upward
creating cloud-shadows
across the landscape.

*Morning dances
constantly changing
the lofty giant's appearance.*

I breathe.
    I become.
        I am.

Communion

— perhaps the healing of the world rests on a shift in our way of seeing, a coming to know that in our suffering and joy we are connected to one another by unbreakable and compelling human bonds. In that knowing, all of us become less vulnerable and alone. The heart, which can see these connections, may be far more powerful a source of healing than the mind.

Rachel Naomi Remen

Once while visiting Trey and Amy when they lived in Decatur, Georgia, I attended an African dance class at the Decatur Community Center. Decatur is a small Atlanta suburb where 30% of the population is African American, many of them refugees or immigrants. I will always remember the sense of hospitality and inclusiveness I felt when I visited there. This memory of attending an African dance class was one of those special times.

The drums sounded a tribal rhythm. Crisp, staccato beats lured me into the moment, mesmerizing me, captivating my awareness, holding me in time. Three black male drummers sat on the old gym stage creating primal, mysteriously haunting beats seeming to emerge from the heart of creation. The speed of the beat increased: faster, faster, faster, then ended abruptly.

Black women dancers moved flowing with ancient drumming patterns, the pink bare soles of their feet pounded smooth varnished floors with purposeful intention.

The dancers were of varying ages, sizes, shapes and heights. Each possessed a unique beauty. Adorned in colorful wraps displaying geometric or floral designs in brilliant hues of blues, oranges, greens, reds and yellows, the fabrics of ankle length skirts swung like an extension of each dancer's body.

Some of the dancers wore turbans and anklets, some were tall and lean and swayed like pine tree saplings moving in the breeze. Some were buxom and muscular, their whole bodies glistening with sweat as they moved in powerful motions.

As the dance drew to conclusion, each performer caught the beat. They moved in unison in vertical lines as if responding to a magnetic force pulling them forward toward a mystical source in the sound. Suddenly, for brief moments, everything blended into one—the drummers, the dancers, the spectators. The dance ended. The performers stopped, caught their breath, hugged each other, laughed and returned to the end of the old gym to begin the dance again.

A few white women and one awkward tall white man attempted the movements with concentrated effort so unlike the natural spontaneity of the black women. The dancers encouraged everyone with welcoming gestures and smiles.

In finale they formed a circle to perform in unison. Then as if touched on the head by a leader in a signal to be "it," a single dancer sensuously dance-stepped to the center to perform solo, then danced out again returning to her place in the circle. At times two women moved to the center dancing as shadows of each other.

I watched in complete presence as my awareness was totally captured by it all. When the rhythms ceased, the dancers collapsed to lie on the coolness of the smooth wood floor.

They stretched and extended their limbs. One sang out in mysterious bird/animal-like tones I sensed arising from a creative center to join everyone there in the great I Am, the Om.

It was a beautiful spring morning. Sitting in an old gym in Decatur, I experienced the hospitality and inclusion from total strangers in an unfamiliar place.

I hold this unexpected gift of community in my heart continually reminding me communion is possible anywhere at any time, forever bearing the promise of peace and enduring joy.

The Dance

*Out beyond my memories and imaginings
there is a wild wonder dancing—dancing,
touching the essence of every living thing
or perhaps it is the essence itself!*

Shadow Dancing

*Morning sunlight
casts her silhouette.
She dances in the dawn.
Arms outstretched,
blowing kisses
she twirls across
the lawn.*

*I wondered
as I watched the show
if it might ever be
that I could love my shadow so
to dance with it
as she.*

Presence

I sense a presence of life itself—
beyond my own existence.
The dawn, the doves, the dog,
all sense it, too,
along with each
arising, living thing—
the grass, the buds, the trees,
and down below the creek
runs free,
tumbling, laughing, delighting
in what it is,
awed by its
own amazing
being!

Slowing

*God has brought you fourth like a plant
and to the earth God will restore you.*

Quran: Noah 71:17-18

I have arrived at a time of the slowing. Elderhood brings us to a place of gradual slowing, not just in physical activity but also of the necessity to be "doing," accumulating, planning for the next event. We enter into a place of being and becoming.

During the past few years I have allowed the young children I teach to guide me in "the power of the slowing," a term Gerald May uses in his book, *The Wisdom of the Wilderness*. On reaching the rangers' station in the Appalachian foothills where he was headed for time alone in the wilderness, he describes confidence in knowing he has been slowed down by a Power. I, too, have been slowed down by the same life force.

I am now at a place in my life where the things I previously identified with—my business, financial security, a home, a particular place in my community no longer identify who I am. Mourning the loss of these identities has opened a new sense of unity and freedom, so that I sense I am continually becoming more fully alive and growing into the richness of full being.

I watch and learn from the young children I teach. I witness their curiosity, their sense of trust and wonder, their connectedness to nature, their enthusiasm for life. I know that I am turning toward home. I am more aware of the difference between having things and experiencing life.

The children teach me not to hurry. I am learning a deeper appreciation for the gift of time for myself and for myself in relationship to others and my surroundings. While working with children, I have discovered our deepest, most meaningful times together have been those in nature—walking trails, wading through streams, following dragonflies, searching for fossils.

I recall a time with my oldest grandson, Jack. Late one afternoon as shadows began descending into Shoal Creek, we walked along the water's edge searching for fossils. While filling our pockets, we discussed how these ancient formations have laid here for centuries. Their existence here and now somehow transported us into participation in a time of long ago.

Later, with pockets bulging we headed back to the car. I began helping Jack remove his muddy shoes. Sitting on the grass, leaning against his elbows, he thoughtfully said to me,

"The Universe is always expanding. Did you know that?"

"Yes, I know," I replied.

"It keeps getting bigger and bigger," he added. "God has a lot of work to do. What does He do when He gets to the end, when there is no more room and He is tired."

"Maybe it is not the end," I answered. "Maybe it is a continual new beginning."

"What color do you think it all is?" I asked him

"I don't know. What do you think?"

"Maybe dark, like a cozy dark, dark with a glow, black silky smooth velvet, comforting and soft," I replied.

"I think it is clear," Jack said.

"Like water?" I questioned.

"Yes, I think everything is clear."

"So you and me, we are clear. God is clear and everything is simply fluid and we are all swimming in it and we are all it."

"Yes," Jack said with the authority of a child. "That's it. Everything is clear."

These are Jack's days of miracles and wonder and also mine. As an elder I want to do all that I can to preserve these experiences in nature for all children here and now and those of future generations.

It is my hope that as elders, my generation can look toward those of our grandchildren and beyond and be purveyors of the wonders of the natural world. As I walk familiar trails, at times I see trash left behind by those who seem to have no reverence, no sense of gratitude for this place they call home, our mother the earth. I witness disheartening effects of drought, tired, stressed trees and plants, dangers I know exist each moment for an outbreak of some uncontrollable fire perhaps carelessly ignited, then fueled by dried undergrowth lying in wait like kindling to feed the flames.

I know we are at a point in history where we cannot reverse climate change greatly contributed to by our own consumption and greed, but may we strive to alleviate its impact. May we attempt to preserve the natural life of our planet so future generations do not look back and ask us: How could you let this happen?

Slowing

*I have come to the time
of the slowing.
The grandmothers' voices
guide me
from forest caves of deep silence,
from earth's center
where sparks of great eruptions dwell.*

*"Keep awake," they say,
"Walk with us,
listen, watch, breathe in
the breath
of time.*

*Slowly, slowly mother with us
that which is now
being born."*

Texas Snow Day

It was not really a snow hill,
simply a slope into the ravine,
a perfect place
for sledding.

Our cardboard box sleds
steadily slid downhill
carving miniature roads
through the snow.

My children's voices sang
through winter silence,

"Come on, Mom.
It's so much fun!"
Laughter rang out
as I fell
face first
into the feathery fluff.

*Tired bodies at day's end,
wet clothes piled at the back door,
steaming hot chocolate in front of a fire—*

*and then next day,
sun.*

Crucifixion

Too many of us today are under the naïve illusion that what is wrong with our world in terms of bitterness and injustice within the system can be fixed simply by fixing the system---without the searing personal change that this demands within even the most minute areas of our lives.

> Ronald Rolheiser, O.M.I.
> The Oblate School of Theology

Friday, November 28, 2008
New York Daily News

A Wal-Mart worker died early Friday after an "out-of-control" mob of frenzied shoppers smashed through the Long Island store's front doors and trampled him, police said.

Crucifixion

"Crucify Him! Crucify Him!" The crowd insisted.
Media and merchants took up the cry
and so it was done!

Jdimytai Damour laid down his life
in the name of meaningless excess and consumption

Cause of death:
asphyxiation due to trampling.

Description of body:
Black male: 34, 6'5", 270 pounds;
black hair, brown eyes.

Description of soul:
According to those who knew him well,
Jdidread, they called him, since he wore
his hair in dreadlocks,
or Jimbo,
was a gentle giant who would have gladly
stepped aside for anyone,
if given the chance.

*Jimbo's great sense of humor
burst forth in smiles
for all he met.
He would engage in conversation
of Japanese Anime or politics with anyone,
any time.*

*Description of employment:
temporary, seasonal, maintenance,
salary: $7.00 an hour*

*That day: Black Friday, 2008, Jimbo was called
for safety's sake to guard the doors
to the temple of goods: Wal-Mart.
Outside a frantic onslaught of consumers
who, in the Holy name of sales goals,
blue rays and high definition tvs
had swelled to a crowd, 2000 and more.*

*At opening time, thunder roared as the temple doors
split in two
and you, Jimbo, were trampled.*

"Forgive us our trespasses!"

*Did you cry out, "My God, my God,
Why have you forsaken me?"
While masses responded, "Crucify him!
We have stood in line for hours!"*

Three sisters and your parents mourn.
They are not alone.
Some of us, Jimbo, recognize
you were the face of
Jesus.

We are enraged!

Lord, we pray that in our haste
we trample not friend or stranger.

Star of Bethlehem we humbly ask
that we be guided
home.

Forgetfulness

Let's begin with this idea, Morrie said. Everyone knows they're going to die but no one believes it... Be compassionate, Morrie whispered. And take responsibility for each other. If we only learned those lessons this would be so much a better place.

> Mitch Ablom
> *Tuesdays With Morrie*

It was late. I was tired and anxious to get home. I had just left the Maundy Thursday service at church. As always it was a moving experience for me.

Imitating Jesus following the Last Supper when he washed the disciples feet, members of the clergy placed a basin of water at the altar and began to wash the feet of those in the congregation wishing to participate. While washing our feet, the priest reminds us to go and do for others what has been done for us.

Now I stood in line at the grocery store checkout counter holding three items. I would not have stopped except that these were items I wanted on hand for the beginning of the following day, particularly the coffee.

At that time of night there was only one checker and a line of about three people ahead of me. I practiced patience. I remembered I can breathe and take time to quiet myself instead of becoming agitated. I no longer want to tire myself by wasting energy on agitation. I stood silently gazing at magazine covers on the rack before me.

Ahead of me I saw a casual acquaintance attempting to pay with a plastic card. Now he was a visibly unhappy customer trying to use the credit card machine. He seemed to take out his irritation on the female checker. He was unpleasant and verbally annoyed. I felt bad for the young employee. She was simply doing her job.

I was reminded of Ellen Bass's poem, "If You Knew." It begins:

"What if you knew you'd be the last
to touch someone?— and goes on to say:

"When a man pulls his wheeled suitcase
too slowly through the airport, when

*the car in front of me doesn't signal,
when the clerk at the pharmacy
won't say Thank you, I don't remember
they're going to die"*

What if the irritated customer had remembered the checkout girl was going to die? What if he'd remembered the people behind him in line were going to die? What if he'd thought to himself, these words and my actions are the last the checker or even one other person around me hears and sees? What if he had acted with pure presence and concern for others rather than reacting from his own self-absorption?

Before I finished checking out myself, a young male store employee stopped to speak to the checkout girl. He said to her, "Good job. I noticed you were using safety methods today when shelving—bending your knees, putting the weight where it needs to be instead of leaning over. When you take care of yourself, you are taking care of us all."

The employee smiled in gratitude. I wondered if someone said or did something kind and loving for this young man earlier in the evening and in so doing sent the unspoken message, "What is done to you, go now and do to others." Perhaps his comments were simply the result of an employee-training program, some incentive plan. I prefer to think the former. I like to imagine he heard the message from someone, somewhere, sometime that I had just heard in the Maundy Thursday readings from John 13:

"I give you a new commandment, that you love one another. Just as I have loved you, you also should love one another."

Holiness

*The Presence
dwells
in each
of us.*

*I forget
that
I am Holy,
everyone is
Holy,
all life is
Holy.
I return to
solitude.*

*There
I remember.*

Writing

For all its frailty and bitterness, the human heart is worthy of your love. Love it. Have faith in it. Both you and the human heart are full of sorrow. But only one of you can speak for that sorrow and ease its burdens and make it sing—word after word after word.

Roger Rosenblatt
Unless It Moves the Human Heart

This is what I have found writers do: find a quiet place, welcome that no one is around, no distractions. As for me I open the sliding glass door behind my desk. I want to invite this natural world inside to present me with words I hope will emerge and fall out onto the paper.

I write to be who I am, not to discover who I am. That will never happen completely. I will always remain a mystery even to myself. I write to be this old woman telling her secrets, her stories, her life. I write to the young ones, the ones who follow, to teach them, to offer them reason to wonder, to hope. In writing I discover my own goodness and that of others. I write to give myself to the world that has given me everything I have needed and more and has loved me unconditionally. I write in humility and gratitude.

Energy ebbs and flows within me like waves on the ocean. As I age, I gradually relinquish physical energy and in this time of the slowing, an opening is created for another energy, that of the cosmos, that of wisdom. I can no longer exhaust myself physically and give the energy of compassion and wisdom the space it needs to grow within me. Aging, like grief and writing, can be a lonely business.

When I wake in the mornings and sit down to write, I am attending to grief and joy at once. I am in that holy middle place. There is something about the solitude, the waiting to see what will happen, the anticipation. Perhaps the words I am leaving now are what, in the end, will make my life worth dying for. It is as when I return time after time to sit on the rock above the river and feel my heart lifting off to touch my boy again and in so doing touch everything.

Flying

At times
I sit on the cliff
above the river
imagining
I will push off
and
fly,
but I don't
as I'm not certain
I can.

In dreams
I float
above earth,
becoming one with
all existence.

One day I will
lift off
and soar.
I know that will happen

if I let go
this fear
I have
of
flying.

Openheartedness

The body repeats the landscape. They are the source of each other and create each other.

Meridel LeSuer, poet

As I write now I think of Taos, New Mexico, and my journey there two days following my son's memorial service in Clarkston, Georgia. My friend drove as I looked out at the rocky foothills on one side and the winding Rio Grande River on the other. In the Sangre de Cristo Mountains, my breath flows easier and my movements are freer.

Traveling with windows opened I heard winter breezes and the river's movement along the ancient riverbed with intimate knowledge of where it was and where its path was leading, a gift of age. I, like the river, have discovered that everything in the path is the path. I, like the river, know I am headed into the mystery where both the river and I will merge to become at one with all existence.

As we rounded a bend, suddenly there it was: The Rio Grande Gorge. I had seen this awesome split in the earth many times before but in that moment I sensed I am it and it is I.

I have visited this place from time to time since childhood. I know the gorge was not formed by the force of a river or ice moving through the earth, but created by two tectonic plates colliding in a continental rift resulting in a wide, deep, rocky gorge allowing The Rio Grande to flow through. The river is a gift of this rift, this split in the earth, providing space for a major waterway in this semi- arid region.

I recognize the gorge as Mother Earth's mirroring of my soul. My heart was split open when my son's life collided with death, unexpectedly and traumatically leaving a rift in my heart so wide and deep that initially there was only a dark, endless void.

As the years have passed now and through love and support of many people and dedication to a practice of silent meditation, gifts of openheartedness, compassion and wisdom have and do flow through my heart. As the river now flows through the rift in the earth, compassion flows through my opened heart in ways I could never have imagined and certainly did not expect.

Late one afternoon on an annual trip to Taos, my friend and I drove to the bridge spanning the Rio Grande Gorge. It is always a ritual for me—each visit a renewal, a new beginning. Driving eastward back toward Taos as afternoon sun bounced off the mountains, we commented on the amazing light show.

On this particular day there was probably nothing different about the aspects of Light, but I had changed as now I seem in some ways to change most every day.

I was not just witnessing millions of particles of light surrounding me. I was not only seeing this phenomenon, I was feeling, tasting, hearing its silence, touching it and it was feeling, tasting, hearing, touching me. I experienced the light in ways I have never been open to before.

Light was flowing in and through me as we danced together in those unexpected moments of deep awareness. I felt my previous fears transformed into the fearlessness that had brought me to this place of home. I have carried the sense of this experience with me since then. Often before I go to sleep at night or on waking in the morning, I am there again, in those moments, in that place.

I have learned that when I am awake, I am open to the oneness of things. I find joy in unexpected moments even in the face of grief. I am able to discover connections so that beauty emerges and the sight of a gorge in the earth is not a reminder of despair but a glimpse of the possibility of a broken heart's ability to hold everything. When I am awake, I am not this or that. I am all of it.

"God breaks the heart again, again and again until it stays open," says the Sufi master. I live with the promise given me through experience that when I am faithful to practices that bring me to remembrance of who I truly am, I move forward toward that which I was created to be.

The Rio Grande Gorge

*Sometimes, like today,
I wake
remembering
the Rio Grande Gorge.*

*How we traveled
the road to Taos,
rounded the curve
to suddenly view
the mammoth chasm.*

*The sun must be rising there now,
awakening the canyon's western edge;
night still lingering in its depths.*

*Moment to moment
everything changes.*

*The great celestial
ball of fire shifts
as the planet rotates*

til directly above the gorge
it fills the rift
with brilliant,
eternal
light.

Taos—Again

Pine trees, stucco fences;
in the distance
mountains
lightly dusted
with snow.

Silence,
day begins.

Break me in two, Lord,
as You break open clouds
so sun shines through
on this magnificent day.

Open my heart
so wide
in unlimited hospitality
it welcomes
everything, without
hesitation.

The School House

I wanted to be there
again last night
as I lay in bed
unable to rest
thinking of things
I didn't cause
and cannot fix.

I wanted to lie there,
propped up
   on elbows,
gazing out at
the dark outline
of the mountain framed
by the star-filled night.

I wanted to smell woody scents
of the one room abode,
as breezes caressed me,
and danced through the room.

I wanted to be in the silence
of evening,
that stillness
filled with night sounds
lullabying me to sleep.

Imagination

Imagination is more important than knowledge. Knowledge is limited. Imagination encircles the world.

Albert Einstein

We are all stardust manifested as who we are here and now. We are part of the constellations and so much more than we can imagine. When we come together in intimacy, true giving and receiving, we send stardust out into the universe never knowing where it will land or the lives it will touch.

Like the Man o f La Mancha, Don Quixote, I often see things through the lens of my imagination. Sometimes I mistake windmills for giants. Each time I arrive at Mable Dodge Luhan House in Taos I am reminded of who I am when I see a drawing of the Man of La Mancha on a large tile blended into the stucco wall near the front door.

Many circular stones are embedded in the pathway to and from the lodge. These formations mirror the unending nature of circles. While the circle seems complete in its turning, it continues on and on like the water wheel image of the Trinity ever refilling, ever emptying to refill and empty again endlessly—an unending field of energy.

I remember how we sit together before the fire in contemplation. In those moments, we experience the sense of our true selves individually and collectively.

We cannot do this work alone. When we leave to go our separate ways— what we have received with and through each other goes out into the world.

This is the gift of each intimate encounter: the gift continues to give. We are blessed by the Cosmic Christ. We fully recognize what falling into love is. Across endless, wide spaces, light swims in, around and through us and all existence. The vision of Taos Mountain through bare winter branches offers an image of the magnificence of life seen more clearly through death itself.

In winter the sleeping tree lifts its branches daily toward the unending sky patiently, confidently awaiting the burst of life that will return again and again. It is here we discover who we are, each in our own uniqueness. It is here we share who we are and become more than each of us could ever be individually. We are surrounded by and witness the magnitude of creation. Opening our hearts and minds, we discover what we are looking for is right before us. We give and receive in such a way that there is no distinction between the two.

We are surprised and astonished! We burst into joy! Joy explodes into gratitude and more gratitude!

We reach out in inclusive, unlimited love healing ourselves, healing each other, healing creation. We feel it in our hands. We hold and release it, the unbroken circle of life, knowing we will return to be filled again and again and again!

The Road

*There is a road
beyond the gate,
across the fields
leading to
    the mountain.*

*Pink clouds brush
the distant peak.
Pine tree silhouettes
etched against the sky,
send light
    bouncing
        off branches.*

*There is strength
in this vision,
    and willingness.*

*Willingness that send us
    out again.
Willingness that
    set us free.*

Glorious Grace

*Some sunrises
appear blazing across the sky
like wildfire.
I saw one like that
not long ago
when waking, I pushed back curtains
to watch the presentation
unravel into day.*

*I thought,
This has to be what grace looks like,
if I could see it.*

*What I really meant was,
I was humbled knowing
I am loved so much
I could be freely given
such a glorious show
of light and colors
it took my breath away.*

Darkness

Hello darkness, my old friend.
I've come to talk with you again.

Paul Simon

My mother, without knowing it, taught me to walk into darkness "acting" unafraid. She sent me out on night chores, like emptying the trash in the alley behind the garage. In the 50s there was very little outdoor lighting. The backyard and alley were dark. My mother was not one for allowing a task to be put off, so there was no possibility of waiting until morning.

I remember reluctantly walking out the back door whistling and singing,

Whenever I feel afraid, I hold my head erect, and whistle
a happy tune so no one will suspect I'm afraid.

Oscar Hammerstein II

all the while glancing from side to side, stepping more rapidly as I walked deeper into the unknown. It was a courageous act, this emptying the trash alone in the dark. I felt relief and a sense of accomplishment when I slammed the trash can lid down tightly and ran back toward the house.

I have read accounts of those who recall the time of being safe, warm and snug in their mother's womb surrounded, immersed and held in darkness, the place of our first existence. Through painful and traumatic efforts of both the mother's and the infant's bodies we emerge and begin our way focusing on the light of life. At certain points on my own journey, my life, as happens in each life, has been plunged again and again into darkness. From this darkness I have always found my way home once more. By facing this emptiness I discover more clearly my own true being, that of others and the world around me.

I am aware that darkness fascinates the young children I teach. It is a source of imagination for them but also a place of anxiety. We must teach them that without darkness we would not be able to see glimmers of light returning again and again, continuously guiding us into greater life. We need to assure the children there is solace and belonging in darkness without which there could be no light. We offer them the gift of resilience they will need to face their own life challenges by guiding them to face their darkness.

The mystic John of the Cross experienced great periods of darkness. He wrote about those times as necessary for discovering again the undying and overwhelming love of the Presence that is the love that connects all. It is our separateness that causes our fear. When we remember we are not alone, we remember it is this great void, this emptiness, this glorious darkness that is the first home of all creation.

Through my own personal experiences and having read accounts of similar incidences of others, I believe there is a resonance within creation that exists through darkness and light. Our silence and our suffering opens us to this resonance that ushers us into unexpected joy.

The dictionary defines resonance, "to sound out together." In physics resonance is defined as the state of a system in which abnormally large vibration is produced in response to external stimulus. The frequency of stimulus is the same or nearly the same as the natural vibration produced in such a state. In other words as I understand this stimulus and response come together in just the right frequency to produce vibration. Through encounters with such phenomena I have been brought to an awareness of something far greater than myself as being in control of and in fact being itself the life force. This is the Presence, steady, assuring and enduring through any and all life situations.

I clearly remember experiencing this "sounding out together." One morning while living on the coast of North Carolina, I was riding my bike across a pasture road. Suddenly I heard or felt something. I cannot be sure which but it caught my full attention so that I stopped and stood still with one foot grounded on earth and the other resting on the high pedal. It was then I knew a pulse was moving right up through me. I knew that this was me and I was this. I have never forgotten that moment.

This resonance of life I have come to know has carried me through many times of darkness, returning me again to the light of assurance and hope. Life continues to teach me that turning toward my darkness and pain awakens me to the cries of the world and is developing within me a greater sense of compassion and connection than I have ever known.

When we learn to wake up and turn toward the dark, we find its power is often hidden in the heart of our pain. Most people do not want to do this. It is simple but not easy to face our pain.

My granddaughter, now 15, had an imaginary friend when she was small. Her friend's name was Skeleton. Skeleton only appeared in the darkness when Ginger was alone. I thought Skeleton to be an interesting name for an imaginary friend.

Skeleton was always there in the dark like a shadow, a supporting beam for Ginger, offering safe and caring companionship. Skeleton seemed to be a light that could move about anywhere quickly so as to be in all places at all times illuminating dark places with love.

Maybe we are all skeletons of our true selves and become whole when we emerge from our dark places. We are born into completion in the places we fear. In walking though our darkness we emerge into the wholeness of community.

In *Dark Night of the Soul,* Gerald May explains that as we face and move through our dark periods of life we gain freedom from attachment and our motives become God's motives expressed through us, free of ego self-determination. I believe we move into full being as we walk through the dark and into participatory love.

Darkness

You return each evening.
I am drawn again into you.
I rest dreaming dreams of who I am.
I sleep within your realm held softly, gently
until I am prepared once more to endure
       the light.

Notes From Cypress Creek

Take a walk alone through the woods
Step lightly on wet leaf trails
winding through corridors
of dark tree trunks
until you reach
a clearing of open
pasture land.

Stand still, be speechless, listen.

You will hear the earth sing.
It is a subtle sound—
quiet, cricket-like
but softer as if barely there,
yet pulsing up into
your soul.

*I cannot sing this song
for you.
You must hear it, know it, claim it
as your own.*

*It is there
singing to you.
Listen.*

Gifts

Whatever we have been given is supposed to be given away again, not kept—the gift must always move.

Lewis Hyde
The Gift

WESTWARD

1.
We began driving westward
through Texas hills.
Above grey clouds teased
with much needed rain,
Passing a hand-lettered sign,
"Pray for Rain,"
we did, but little fell.
Out on the plains the cloudless sky
touched earth in every direction.
Cradled in the vastness of creation
we looked out on endless fields

*of cotton and hay
harvested and neatly stacked.*

*Elevation 4,000 feet a marker read.
On the far horizon mountains,
we strained to reach,
appeared as promises
in the distance.*

2.
"*Just head straight out. You will see*
the turn to I-40. You can't miss it,"
the woman at the motel desk
in Roswell, N.M,. explained.

147 miles later we discovered
she was right.
Out on the plains, wide spaces of earth,
and sky, beginning-less and endless,
distance and time have other meanings

Frequently along the way
a blackbird or two led us
from one landmark to the next
until we finally reached the ramp
to emerge onto the interstate.

Immediately a billboard
grabbed my attention.
"You can change the story,"
it announced.
So the possibilities, I pondered,
are endless even now, old girl,
as you journey on.

3.
Snow patches linger on rocky ridges,
crosses mounted on random peaks,
The Continental Divide,
elevation: now 6,000 feet,
Ship Rock, the Zuni Nation,
The Petrified Forest,
The Painted Desert,
San Francisco Peaks,
all in the drive from Albuquerque, N.M.
To Flagstaff, Az.

I am here now,
tired but filled with memories.

4.
Whoa! Stop!
The sign at the beginning of the trail read
and listed specific instructions:

There are many steps ahead
and steep drop-offs.
Pace yourself.
Know your limits.

We began the descent into Walnut Canyon
headed back into time to a place
where Hopi Indians carved out dwellings
in high cliffs along the riverbed.

There were many markers along the way.
One read, "Hopis build their houses
close to each other to remind them
they are suppose to love each other.
When a man decided to build a house,
he gathered materials provided by nature
and drew from his reserve of goodwill
(and that of his relatives)
among his clan and friends,
acquired from his own participation
in such cooperative projects."

Now is the time.
We must return to this way of living.

5.
I am here again on the desert.
"The desert will lead you to
your heart where I will speak,"
the scripture says.

Sunlight inches along its path
until it hides behind the mountain.
Giant Saguaro cactus
surround the outdoor chapel
where I sit alone.

Desert breezes dance,
shadows lengthen,
quietly I wait for the glow
of the first evening star.

Relationship

The balance comes in less is more—in relationship we complete ourselves.

from a homily

These quotes are from a homily presented by a young priest on Grandparents Day at St. Andrew's School in Austin, Texas. It was Holy Wednesday, the Day of Betrayal.

I have reflected on the word betrayal, wondering how much over my lifetime that word has applied to me. How much of my own betrayals do I want to recall or do I prefer to deny?

Looking back on my life I see truth in the fact that there is balance in less is more: fewer words, less judgment, less accusation, less criticism, less manipulation, less denial. All would mean more listening, more understanding, more sharing, more openness, more compassion and more peace.

"In relationship we complete ourselves" are words that remind me I am never separate. I am never who I

am completely without relationship, beginning with my relationship to myself.

I sat in a meditation group I attend regularly early on Ash Wednesday morning. Following silence we read together an article on aging. Since I am only 75 (the article stated that anyone under 80 was still "only" a certain age), I explained my experience of releasing butterflies with my three-year-old preschool class.

Together the children and I created a habitat and daily observed the metamorphosis from caterpillars to chrysalises to butterflies. I shared the beauty of the moment of releasing the butterflies. The children waved their arms and ran fluttering behind the miraculous creatures. I will not forget the joy of the experience.

Before meditation I discussed with another member of the group my persistent desire to let go of possessions at this point in my life and of having reached a realization that things I once thought important to possess are actually not so meaningful now. She told me about the Peace Pilgrim.

Later I looked up the Peace Pilgrim: Mildred Norman Ryder, July 18, 1908 to July 7, 1981. She was a nondenominational spiritual teacher, a mystic, a pacifist, and a peace activist.

Her pilgrimage began in 1953 in Pasadena, Ca., and continued for 28 years. She had no backing, no money and asked for nothing. She walked more than 25,000 miles for peace and vowed to "remain a wanderer until mankind has learned the way of peace, walking until given shelter and fasting until given food."

She wrote: *"In order for the world to become more peaceful, people must become more peaceful. Among mature people war would not be a problem, it would be impossible. In their maturity people want at the same time, peace and things which make war. However, people can mature just as children grow up. Yes, our institutions and our leaders reflect our immaturity, but as we mature we will elect better leaders and set up better institutions It always comes back to the thing so many of us wish to avoid: working to improve ourselves."*

Following the thread of this day left me with these thoughts—balance: less is more; we become who we are in relationship; we cannot want peace and at the same time want things which make war; we must work to improve ourselves. It is time to grow up. I realize I have lived more maturely when I have given up my notion of wanting peace and at the same time harbored those things that make war.

Isn't peace what we all want to celebrate? I asked myself at the close of Ash Wednesday: are we willing to surrender our denial, our self-justification, to acknowledge our betrayals and move forward in compassion? Can we learn to embrace our differences and find connections with and in each other? Can we give up those things in ourselves that cause war? Can we for the sake of our children and grandchildren and the miracle of butterflies now grow up and turn toward the resurrection? Can we acknowledge the Christ consciousness that brought us together and that we will never fully experience until we look intimately into the eyes of others and remember: It was Christ all along. It was Christ. It was peace all along. It was peace.

Resurrection

*I have taken you back
into my body
to birth you
again.*

*As sunflowers drop seeds,
gifts returned to earth
to bear beauty anew
as each oncoming wave
touches shore,
then returns to be enfolded
by the sea,*

*so I have taken
you back, my son,
to send you forth again.*

*Together we will dance
in fields of
resurrection.*

Robashin

I learned that I can only recover myself when I keep them near. If I distance myself from them, and their absence, I am fractured. I am left feeling I've blundered into a stranger's life.

> Sonali Deranlyagala
> *Wave*, a memoir

When I began writing this, I told myself writing about the unexpected death of my son, Trey, was done when I finished my book, *Blackbird Fly!* I told myself, "no one wants to hear any more about this," but as I have continued writing I realize this traumatic event and my own near-death experience eleven months prior are the lens through which I now view my life. These events are a major part of who I am now.

Robashin in Japanese means Grandmother or Grandmother Mind—big mind, open mind, compassionate mind. From my moments in the cradle of shock, the insulation, that something that kept me immobile in my grief when I needed to be—when I was immersed in that state of disbelieving and at the same time propelled into doing things others called courageous—something much bigger was breathing, speaking, moving for me and flowing through me.

This presence has brought me to a place where I can now continue to move into the fullness of Grandmother Mind. Zen Master Dogen wrote frequently of the importance of developing the attitude of *Robashin* which brings forth in one selflessness, caring and loving concern for others. Dogen, in fact, instructed his student, Gikai, that to develop in this way was imperative and all of one's tasks should be performed with this attitude.

It is my intent as I progress further into elderhood that I develop this Grandmother Mind. In order to do that, I remember that without those who have gone before me, I am not complete. In their absence I continually learn to find them everywhere always loving and supporting me on my path.

Blessings

The iron bell tower stood near the kitchen door outside the farmhouse. At mealtimes Tom rang it until we all came running from the barn, the nearby pasture, the play yard and down the dusty road. Whatever we were doing we knew it was time to stop and be present at the table. My grandfather and grandmother stood by their chairs at each end of the table waiting for us to gather. When my cousins, my mother, my aunt and I had taken our places, my grandfather pulled back his chair signaling the family to be seated. We bowed our heads, held hands and prayed together, then passed around the noonday meal of fresh produce straight from the land. We talked and laughed—three generations of family sharing together a daily act of communion.

Heart Home

Three large windows
framed the bed.
I stood looking out at
great shade trees growing on
the sloping lawn.
I thought—I could stay right here.

"She said it was the nicest house
she ever lived in,"
my friend explained,
speaking of her mother—
the one who woke
each morning,
went to bed
each night,
then finally died
in this room.

I thought—
this is what she meant
as I stared
out the window
at the trees.

Miss Essie
(My grandmother)

In my heart I hold:
her smile,
her twinkling eyes,
her dimpled cheeks,
her open arms,
her contemplative sound
as she sat in her chair rocking,
lips puckered producing
a whisper-whistle repeating
again and again
what seemed to be
an inviting,
"You-we, You-we,"
    comforting
        and inclusive.

The Cottonwood Tree

The cottonwood tree in our backyard grew so tall I was sure it was the tallest cottonwood ever! Its leaves rustled in breezes, tossing their silver undersides into view. My children played for hours beneath its branches. On starlit nights when everyone was sleeping I sat on the back steps gazing at the tree as I talked to it, sang to it, told it my innermost longings. We had a relationship, the cottonwood tree and I. Years passed and everything changed. The children grew up. Their father and I divorced. We sold the family home. Whenever I return to the city, I stop to see the place. Most everything seems the same, except the cottonwood tree no longer stands. Someone cut it down, killed my friend; murder in the first degree. When my children, as young adults, discovered the crime, they asked me how anyone could do such a thing, expecting me to somehow have an answer. I, who always had some seemingly logical explanation, was at a loss for words!

Family Stars

I remember you, Trey, how as soon as you burst through the door at the end of the day you grabbed your guitar and began to play. No matter what we were doing we stopped to join in—baby Alice Elizabeth twirling like a top and me singing like a star—fulfilling my every dream!

Intensity

*My son's baseball caps sit
on the old wood trunk.
I see them daily,
recall him grab one,
head to the door,
call out,
"Come on, Mom, we'll be late!"
and my reply,
"Wait! Do I have everything?"
"If you don't, it doesn't matter.
Just come on, Mom,
we don't want to miss anything!"*

Spring Break

1.
*Sitting watching sunrise
on the ocean,
morning light twinkles
on the horizon,
overhead bird migrations,
one flock, then another,
V formations
headed north.
How do they do that?
How do they know
when, where?
Some inner guidance
calls them.
They follow
without hesitation.*

2.
*Early morning voices,
Please not yet!
"Can we go to the beach?"
"Too early, loves."*

Lingering waning moon,
"Look there's daddy!"

3.
"Look!" the child said,
holding out her finger
where a tiny moth perched.
"It likes me a lot."
"I know," I said.
"Still,
we should find it a leaf.
It can't live
       with you
             forever."

Almost Home

*Standing
at the front door
waiting.
I look inside
      at the
          stairway,
the altar-like table
against the wall
bearing sacred tokens
collected through
the years.*

*Peering
down the
hallway
I glimpse
 the corner
of the kitchen
      table.*

*Suddenly I long to be there,
sitting unhurried,
saying whatever
comes to me
or nothing
at all.*

What If

*What if
at the moment
I recalled the vision
of my son
receiving CPR,
his unresponsiveness,
his great heart
stopped
forever?*

*What if,
at that moment
of recollection,
I had not looked down,
to compose myself
enough
to speak?*

*What if
instead,
I had looked
into your eyes,
been fully seen
suffering,
weak,
afraid?*

What would have happened next?

*What did I fail
to give and receive
when
I looked
away?*

At Seventy-Five

*I have awakened now
for seventy-five years,
opened my eyes,
to a new day.*

*Looking back,
each day
has been good,
including those
I did not think
I wanted—*

*Even the dark one
have been my teachers.*

*This day I wake
fully alive
to light inching
it's way above
the hill.*

This day sunbeams
illuminate
each moment.

This day
I cherish
and the next
    and each day yet
to be granted me
    here,
        now.

This day
I bow to life—
all of it
and say,

Thank You,
    Thank you!

Aug. 29, 2014

The Archer

—everything holds

my sorrow.

I sense

an ancient warrior

pull his bowstring taut

then release a single arrow—

sending me

into the scalding

light.

With deep gratitude,
Judy Beene Myers

Acknowledgments

I am grateful to my editor, Gerald Tilma, of the Undergraduate Writing Center at The Universtiy of Texas, who has made my task of writing somewhat less fearful. Gerald quietly met me with encouraging words and offered his unfailing assurance of assistance in completion of this writing project.

I am grateful to my writing teacher, Elizabeth Harper Neeld, who introduced me to a creative process that I could truly call mine and who taught me that no matter how busy I seem to be there is always time for my writing project if I "just do something every day."

I am grateful to Appamada, a center in Austin for contemporary Zen practice led by my teachers, Flint Sparks and Peg Syverson. This sangha is a home to me— a constant place for meditation practice and inquiry. Without Appamada I do not believe I could have returned to life fully after the death of my son. As a Christian, my experience with Appamada for the past 10 years has deepened my relationship with my own faith tradition.

I am grateful to Cassie Weyandt, photographer and Appamada sangha member, who designed this book cover. I am grateful to Laurie Winnette, also a sangha member, whose hands are in the photograph and represent to me the hands of Appamada, all of which have and continue to hold me. I am grateful to Rick Wright, another sangha member, who at the last minute agreed to take on the task of final copy editing. I am grateful to Virginia Hagerty who voluntarily offered to proof read my manuscript.

The name Appamada comes from traditional Pali language and is translated as *mindful care* or *watchful concern* which, particularly regarding my experiences of the past five years, it has proven to embody.

I am grateful to photographer Lenny Foster of Living Light Studio in Taos, New Mexico, for the gift of the photograph used as the background for my opening poem, *Flexibility*. There are people in your life you know you are destined to meet and for me Lenny is one of those people. His spirituality and connection with life is exhibited in his photographic work and can be explored at LennyFoster.com.

I am grateful to my readers Paula D'Arcy, Jolynn Free, Judy Knotts and Carolyn Scarborough, for their time, their thoughtfulness and continuing encouragement.

And as I said in the preface I am grateful to my Writing Community for what we have each accomplished individually and have meant to each other as a community.

A bow, Judy Beene Myers

Made in the USA
Columbia, SC
03 May 2017